Chip Carving Patterns

Wayne Barton

Sterling Publishing Co., Inc.   New York

This book is lovingly dedicated to the memory of my parents, Bruce B. and Ruth L. Barton, who always had faith in their son.

Library of Congress Cataloging-in-Publication Data

Barton, Wayne.
    Chip carving patterns / Wayne Barton.
        p.   cm.
    ISBN 0-8069-5782-4
    1. Wood-carving. 2. Wood-carving—Patterns. I. Title.
TT199.7.B36   1990
736′.4—dc20
                                                                                89-26174
                                                                                CIP

Copyright © 1990 by Wayne Barton
Published by Sterling Publishing Co., Inc.
387 Park Avenue South, New York, N.Y. 10016
Distributed in Canada by Sterling Publishing
% Canadian Manda Group, P.O. Box 920, Station U
Toronto, Ontario, Canada M8Z 5P9
Distributed in Great Britain and Europe by Cassell PLC
Artillery House, Artillery Row, London SW1P 1RT, England
Distributed in Australia by Capricorn Ltd.
P.O. Box 665, Lane Cove, NSW 2066
Manufactured in the United States of America
All rights reserved

CONTENTS

INTRODUCTION

Chip carving has embraced a multitude of motifs, interpretations, and adaptations through the centuries. This certainly would indicate that it is a fluid art form and one within the range of capabilities, talents, and enjoyable pursuits of many people. With more leisure time on their hands than ever before, those who are inclined to carve are happily discovering chip carving in numbers that give rise to a renaissance.

There are several reasons for chip carving's growing popularity today. One is that chip carving is the fastest, easiest, and simplest way there is to carve. The tools are few and the technique is quite basic. Another reason is that being a decorative form of carving, it has a wide application. Most important, it is a type of carving that most anyone can do with pleasing results.

This book is a design effort. Unlike my previous book, *Chip Carving Techniques & Patterns,* also published by Sterling, which is more instructionally oriented, this book focuses on designs and how they can be developed.

The book is not representatively definitive. Chip carving cuts across many cultures and centuries that have contributed to a vast array of design possibilities. It is hoped that this book will play a role in the continuing development of chip-carving designs for future generations.

Having studied in Switzerland, I must confess that many of the designs in this book bear a strong Swiss influence, although all are not representative of that particular style. In fact, some designs are very different from those that are recognized as belonging to the Swiss genre. However, because Swiss chip carving has a lyrical style that is vibrant with movement, rhythm, and balance, it does offer much from which we can all benefit.

Most of the pieces shown in this book are accompanied by the primary line drawings (patterns) from which they are carved. These drawings have neither shading nor embellishment so that you can easily trace or photocopy them, or change their sizes with a photocopying machine. Comparing the carving drawing with the photo of the carving will help you understand what and how to carve.

In order to get the correct proportions and balance of a design translated into a carving, it's helpful to make a complete picture of the carving on paper first. It is easy to become confused and overwhelmed by the size or complexity of a chip carving. But by making a drawing first, you can break down a complex carving into its components, and it will become much simpler to understand. Design is the way we define space, and how we resolve that definition becomes our carving.

Eliminating the dark mystery of design sheds light upon the entire carving process. It is with this purpose in mind that this book has been written.

TOOLS AND MATERIALS

One of the pleasures of chip carving is the limited number of tools and materials that is needed to do a complete job. And, unlike some other forms of carving, acquiring additional tools will not increase your skill nor produce a better finished product.

All of the carvings shown in this book were executed with only two knives (see Illus. 1). Made in Switzerland, they are the finest knives on the market today for chip carving, and are manufactured with the same high quality and precision for which all Swiss tools have become famous. It is necessary to have knives of this quality with these strong handles and blade configurations in order to make deep, curved cuts safely and accurately in a single pass. This will give your work a smooth, sharp appearance, which typifies excellent chip carving. More potential carvers have become discouraged as a result of initially trying to carve with the wrong tools that were improperly sharpened than by any other factor.

Fortunately, these chip-carving knives are available throughout North America and Europe. They are manufactured by Klotzli and have a "WB" logo on the handle. These are the same knives used in Swiss carving schools and carried by Swiss shops. After many years of carving and trying other knives, these are the only ones I recommend.

The two Swiss chip-carving knives are quite different from each other in shape and use. The #1 knife is called a cutting knife and is used for any cuts that result in the removal of wood or chips. The #2 knife is referred to as a stab knife and removes no wood at all. Instead, it is used for decorative purposes, and makes a wedge-shaped mark or incision by cutting the wood fibres and spreading them permanently at the same time. This knife, though not used as frequently as the other, is extremely important. It makes its own designs and enhances the carving executed by the cutting knife. The two knives complement each other very nicely.

Once you have the two correct carving knives, you'll need to sharpen them and keep them sharp. There are as many devices for sharpening as there are ways to do so. In my previous book, *Chip Carving Techniques & Patterns,* I suggested the use of flat, hard Arkansas stones. However, true hard Arkansas stones have become difficult to find and are expensive. Today I use and recommend only flat ceramic sharpening stones for several good reasons. First, they are so hard that no matter how much you use them, they will remain absolutely flat. This is important for keeping the cutting edges of the knives straight. Also, unlike natural stones in which quality will vary from one stone to another, the high quality of flat ceramic sharpening stones remains constant because they are manufactured. Secondly, ceramic stones need no oil or water as a lubricant for the sharpening process. This makes sharpening a much less messy process. Most importantly, flat ceramic stones will sharpen and polish your knives to a mirror finish, which is essential for clean, crisp carving.

You will need only two ceramic sharpening stones and both are

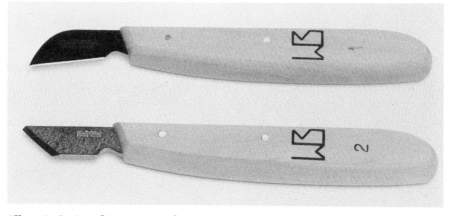

Illus. 1. Swiss chip-carving knives.

necessary. One is a medium-grade, which is used first for shaping and sharpening the blade. The other is an ultra-fine and is used for polishing the blade and keeping the edge freshly sharp. Once your blade is sharp and polished, just the ultra-fine stone is needed to keep it that way. In a day's carving, depending on the type of wood you are using and how much work is done, you will need to freshen the blade only once or twice.

Sharpening the two knives at the correct angle is imperative. The #1 cutting knife is sharpened at an approximate 10° angle or less. You can determine this angle by raising the knife off the stone no more than the space that would accommodate a dime under the back edge of the blade (see Illus. 2). This angle is a maximum. In many cases, you may have to sharpen the #1 knife at an even flatter angle. Proper angling is extremely important in order to have the blade flow through the wood smoothly and easily. The #2 stab knife is sharpened at approximately 30°, which is about what the factory-established angle is on a new blade.

Illus. 2. Raise the #1 cutting knife off the sharpening stone no more than what it takes to insert a dime under the back edge of the blade.

The remainder of the tools needed for chip carving are a pencil (a mechanical one with a .05 lead size works well), ruler, eraser, and a drafting-type compass (Illus. 3). Use a grade "B" lead for both the compass and pencil. This softer-grade lead makes legible lines without impressing the wood, and it is easier to clean off than harder grades of lead. When it's time to clean excess pencil marks off your carving, you'll find an ink eraser does it quickly and neatly.

All of the carvings shown in this book are executed in basswood, butternut, and eastern white pine. These woods, particularly bass-

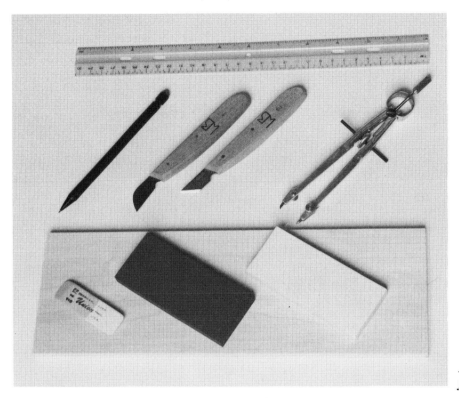

Illus. 3. Tools needed for chip carving.

wood (also known as linden or lime), are exceptionally well suited for chip carving, although they are not the only ones that carve well.

The tools and materials recommended and shown in this book, including the basswood plates and boxes, are generally available from most wood-carving suppliers. Should you have any difficulty finding them, however, contact me for some specific suppliers at the Alpine School of Woodcarving, Ltd., 225 Vine Avenue, Park Ridge, IL 60068 (807/692-2822).

Helpful Hints

Many times when a carver is just beginning, things don't always go as planned or seem as easy as originally considered. (This phenomenon is not limited to beginners.) It may be that the actual carving doesn't appear correct, or there may be a problem with the design. Perhaps it is the process of laying out the work that is awkward. Eventually, everyone experiences one problem or another. Here are a few hints that will make your carving easier, more accurate, and professional-looking. With a little practice, anyone can master them.

1. For a good contrast of light and shadow, make your cuts or chips at a 65° angle in the wood (see Illus. 4).
2. When making curved cuts, stand the knife up (see Illus. 5). The tighter or smaller the curve, the more perpendicular the knife must be to the carving. It is impossible to drag an excess amount of metal around a curve without producing a chatter or choppy appearance. However, the 65° angle at which the blade is inserted into the wood to scribe the wall of the chip does not change.
3. Clean your chips out as you carve. Don't leave little bits of wood in the bottom of your cuts. Your work should appear clean and crisp.

4. To carve straight lines successfully, train your eye always to look ahead of the blade. Never look at the blade itself and don't use a straightedge as a guide. In a short time, you will be making straight lines quicker than you imagined possible.

5. Make all cuts only as deep as necessary to remove a chip. Avoid excessive undercutting that might remove wood that you wanted to remain.

6. Making crescent-shaped chips where curved lines are drawn will add a fullness or a three-dimensional appearance to a carving. This is particularly true for free-form designs (see Illus. 6 and 7).

7. Vary and combine geometrical shapes in a carving for a look of life and vitality. Using the same chip (particularly the three-cornered chip) may be mechanically correct but is artistically very dull.

8. Don't overcarve a piece. In most cases, the area you leave uncarved is as important as what you do carve. It will help "show" the work.

9. When two tapered chips of the same shape must be brought to a single point (see Illus. 8), you will be able to keep the center ridge straight and unbroken if you bring only one chip all the way to the center and hold the second back slightly. This is especially true when cutting cross grain.

10. It is best to draw your design directly on the wood. All lines that can be drawn with a straightedge or compass should be done this way. Because most pieces vary in size, drawing directly on the wood will allow you to proportion your work accurately. In some cases, it will be easier to space free-form designs properly on a piece or within a larger design if you

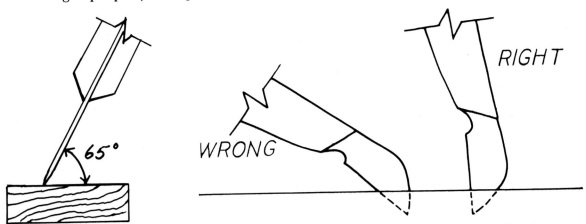

Illus. 4 (left). The #1 cutting knife is properly inserted in the wood at a 65° angle. Illus. 5 (right). When making curved cuts, stand the knife perpendicular to the wood.

Illus. 6. Pattern.

Illus. 7. For a three-dimensional effect, make curved chips crescent shaped in free form.

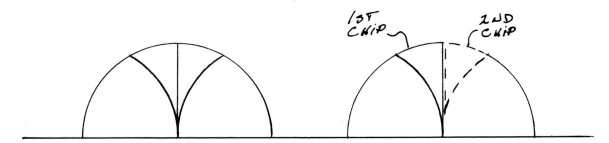

Illus. 8. Two tapered chips of the same shape brought to a single point.

trace them from a predrawn sketch. When tracing, use graphite paper, which cleans off wood like an ordinary pencil. Regular carbon paper is greasy and difficult to remove. For easy final cleaning of pencil and tracing marks, use an ink eraser.

Here's a neat trick. You can transfer any single-line drawing, or pattern, to wood by simply making a photocopy of it, placing the copy face down on the wood, and ironing it. The heat will drop the drawing from the paper to the wood. This technique also works well with transferring letters if you first make a transparency. Turn the transparency so that the lettering is copied backwards on regular paper. Then, when you place the paper face down on the wood, the letters will come out correctly.

BORDERS

In any carving, the border usually sets the tone or feel of the carving. It may be a single line or intricate enough to render the carving complete. The borders shown in Illus. 9–13 are by no means the entire spectrum of possibilities for chip carving. They do represent, however, the very simple to the difficult, from the basic three-cornered chip (1–3 and 7 in Illus. 10) to the complexly convoluted paisley (14 in Illus. 12). Though all of the borders here are drawn on a curve, they work just as successfully when executed on a straight line.

Note the different feeling the simple three-cornered-chip border gives when its direction is reversed (1 and 2 in Illus. 10), or combined with a scallop (5). Note also that the heart border (11 in Illus. 12) is made only of slightly modified, small three-cornered chips on top and larger ones on the bottom. The paisley border (14) is entirely drawn with a compass.

Illus. 9. Box lid of 21" x 10" butternut.

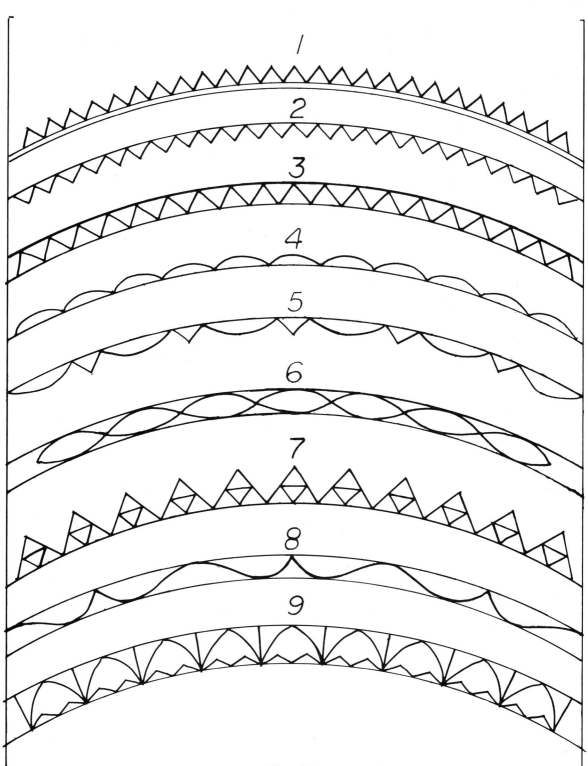

Illus. 10.

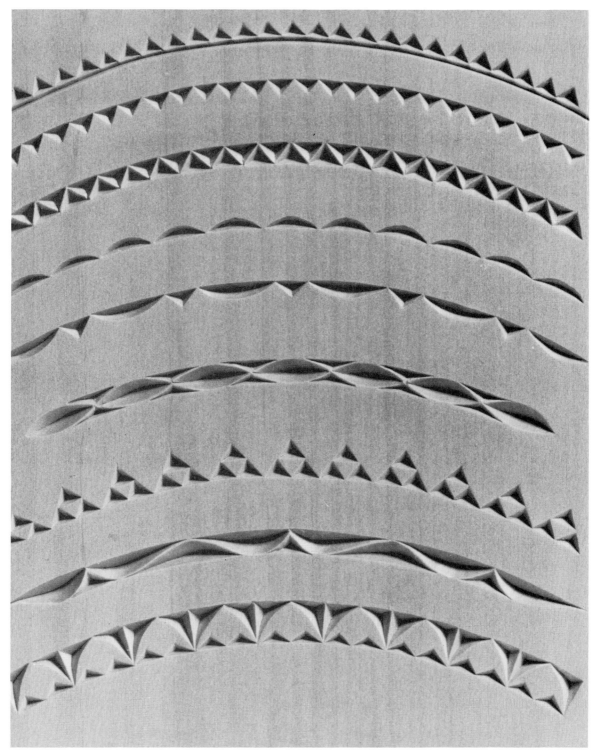

Illus. 11. Border designs.

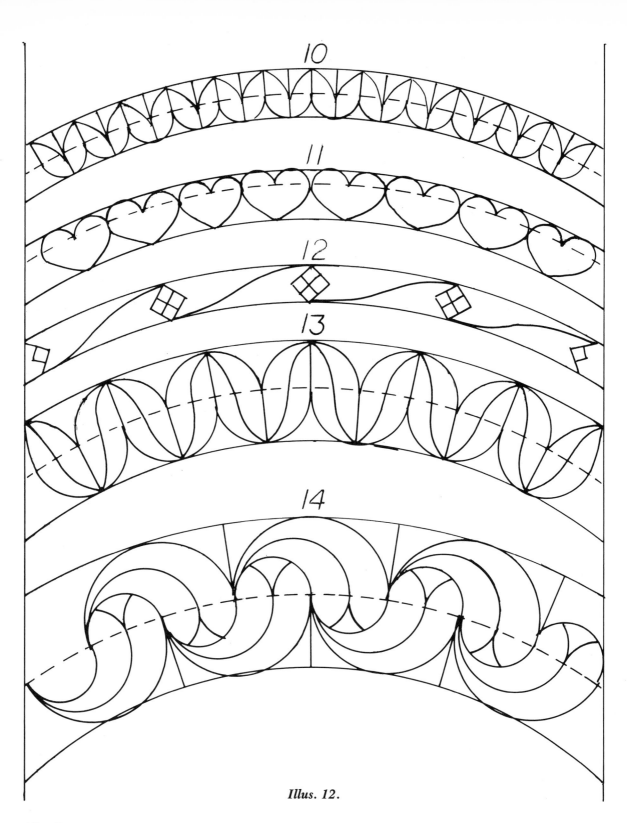

Illus. 12.

Illus. 13. Border designs.

SCULPTURED EDGES

One little-known aspect of chip carving involves taking a basic geometric shape, such as a square or rectangle, and transforming it into a decorative piece. This is accomplished by giving the shape what is called sculptured edges. By cutting any combination of notches and scoops in the edges of the wood, you can give a piece the appearance of taking on another form or shape. Applying this little carving trick will extend your design possibilities. See Illus. 14–17 for various examples.

Illus. 14. Scalloped edges on a chip-carved, 11" x 17", basswood address plate.

Illus. 15. Ornately chip-carved scalloped edges on a 2½" x 6½" white pine box.

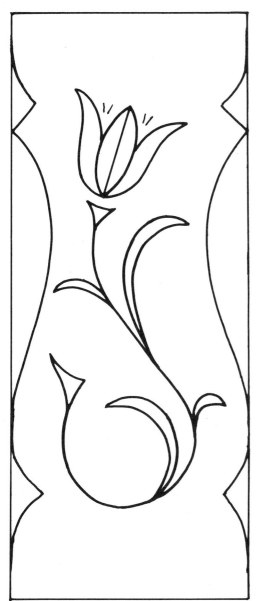

Illus. 16.

Illus. 17. A corbel of 5" x 7" basswood with chip-carved edges.

ROSETTES

One of the most popular (as well as traditional) aspects of chip carving is the making of rosettes. There are rosettes in nearly every style. You can use bold, deep cuts to create a piece that resembles a Gothic rose window, or small, delicate chips to create a lace-doily pattern. The design possibilities are endless.

Looking at the completed carving of a rosette can be a bit intimidating because of its apparent complexity. But when seen as a simple line drawing, it can be more readily understood. When the line drawing (or pattern) and the finished work are juxtaposed, all chip carving takes on clarity.

As you look at the photos in this section, separate the rosettes from the borders. Isolating the various components of a work also helps to clarify its design.

Illus. 18.

Illus. 19. Basswood 8"-diameter plate.

Illus. 20.

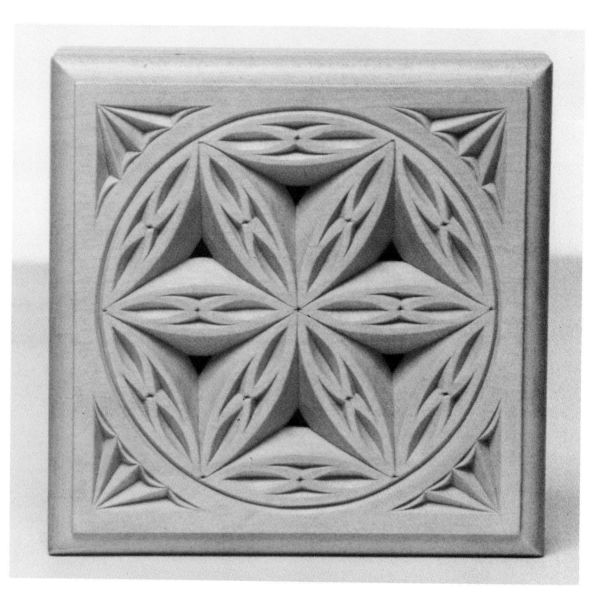

Illus. 21. Pierced lid for a 5" x 5" x ³⁄₈", chip-carved, basswood box.

Illus. 22.

Illus. 23. Swiss lace 4"-diameter rosette.

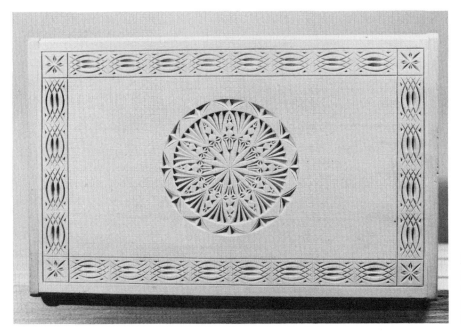

Illus. 24. Box lid with Swiss lace rosette and triple-lace border carved in 13" x 8½" basswood.

Illus. 25.

Illus. 26. Basswood 10"-diameter plate.

Illus. 27.

Illus. 28. Basswood 8"-diameter plate (design by Robert Ostmann).

Illus. 29.

Illus. 30. Basswood 10″-diameter plate.

Illus. 31.

Illus. 32. Basswood 12"-diameter plate.

Illus. 33.

Illus. 34. Plate with six-point rosette and floral border—of 10"-diameter basswood.

Illus. 35.

Illus. 36. Plate with a locking-rings rosette and egg-and-dart border—of 8″-diameter basswood.

Illus. 37.

Illus. 38. Basswood 14"-diameter plate with paisley rosette.

Illus. 39.

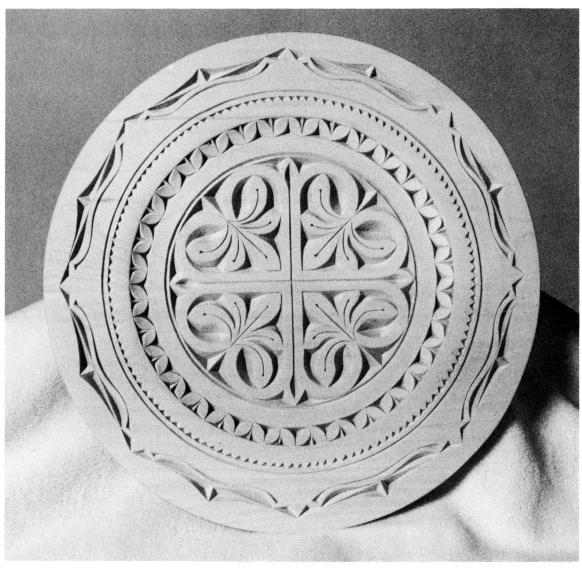

Illus. 40. Basswood 10"-diameter plate.

Illus. 41.

Illus. 42. Basswood 14"-diameter plate.

Illus. 43.

*Illus. 44. Basswood
14"-diameter plate.*

Illus. 45.

Illus. 46. Box lid of 9½" x 7" basswood.

Illus. 47.

Illus. 48. Basswood 14" - diameter plate.

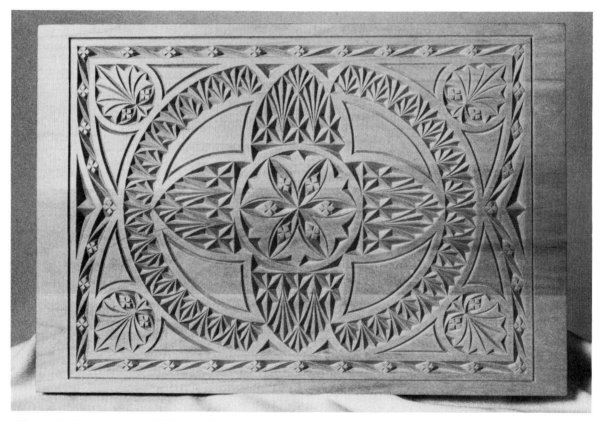

Illus. 49. Wall plaque of 12" x 18" basswood.

FREE-FORM MOTIFS

The traditional free-form motifs found in Switzerland (and other European countries) are those with which the people are familiar in their everyday lives, and many have a symbolic significance. These motifs include the predominance of flowers and birds (and in the canton of Bern, the bear). They are not, however, the only motifs that adapt well to chip carving. Nearly all natural forms, objects, and scenes can be translated into chip carving, and can be represented in realistic, stylized, or abstract ways. Probably more than any other type of chip carving, free form offers a carver the greatest opportunity for self-expression because nature can be portrayed by such a wide variety of interpretations. Various free-form motifs follow.

Illus. 50.

Illus. 51. Grizzly bear and border executed entirely with the #2 stab knife on an 8"-diameter basswood plate (design by Vard Porter).

Illus. 52.

Illus. 53. Dandelion carved in basswood—4" high.

Illus. 54.

Illus. 55. Canadian maple leaf.

Illus. 56. Canadian fleur-de-lis.

Illus. 57.

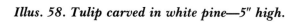

Illus. 58. Tulip carved in white pine—5″ high.

58   <small>FREE-FORM MOTIFS</small>

Illus. 59.

Illus. 60. Thistle carved in white pine—5" high.

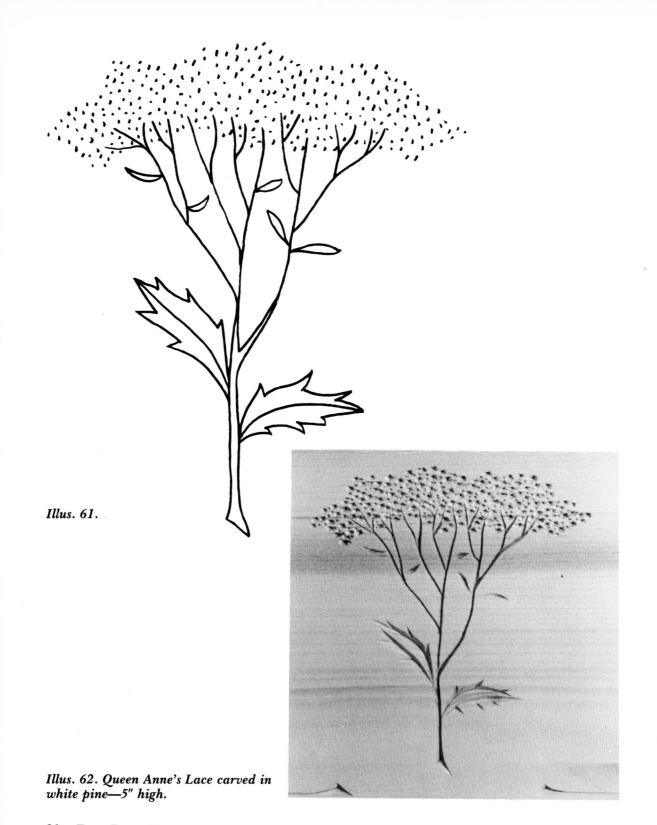

Illus. 61.

Illus. 62. Queen Anne's Lace carved in white pine—5" high.

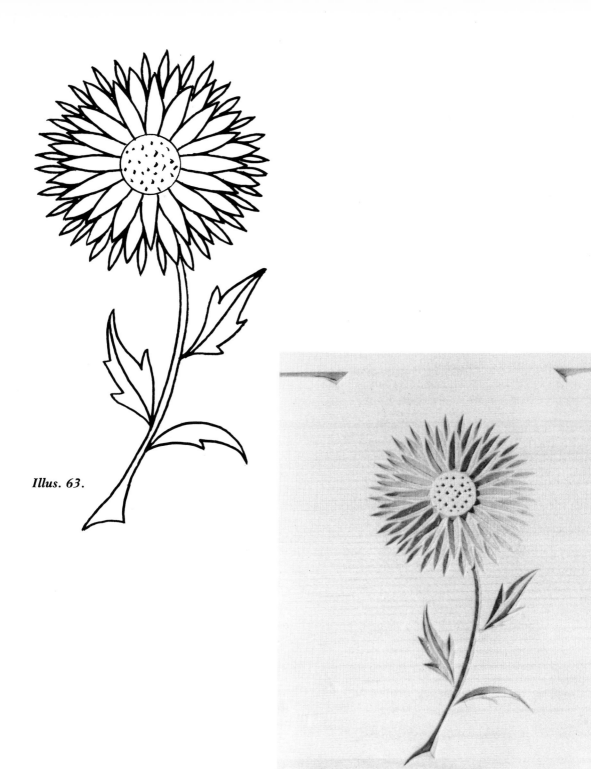

Illus. 63.

*Illus. 64. Zinnia carved in white pine—
5″ high.*

Illus. 65.

*Illus. 66. Edelweiss carved in white
pine—5" high.*

Illus. 67.

Illus. 68. Lily-of-the-valley carved in white pine—5" high.

Illus. 69.

Illus. 70. Corbel with six-point rosette and floral design—of 17" x 17" white pine.

Illus. 71.

Illus. 72. Floral bouquet—of 16"-diameter basswood.

Illus. 73.

Illus. 74. Butterboard of 7" x 13" basswood.

Illus. 75.

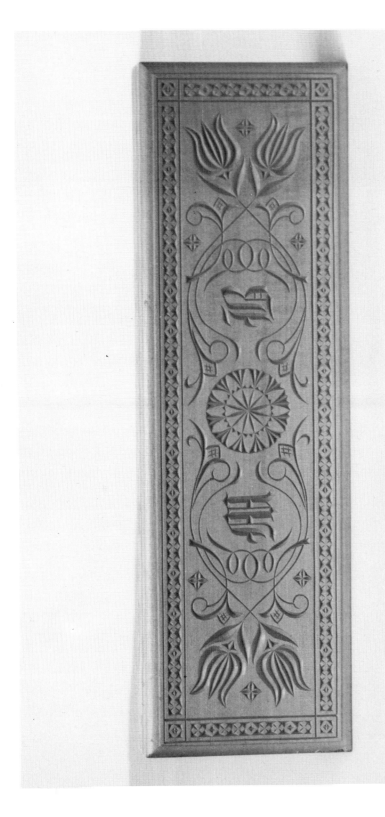

Illus. 76. Knitting-needle box with 12-point rosette and floral pattern—of 5" x 16" basswood.

Illus. 77.

Illus. 78.

Illus. 79. Box lid with floral design and double-diamond border—of 9½" x 7" basswood.

Illus. 80.

Illus. 81. Wall plaque with the four seasons carved in 18"-diameter basswood (photo by Martin Vogel).

Illus. 82.

Illus. 83. Box front panel—of 5" x 12" basswood.

Illus. 84.

Illus. 85. Box rear panel—of 5" x 12" basswood.

Illus. 86.

Illus. 87. Box side panel—of 5" x 7½" basswood.

Illus. 88.

78   FREE-FORM MOTIFS

Illus. 89. Wedding plate with love birds and egg-and-dart border, dated 1987—14"-diameter basswood.

Illus. 90. Lid of wedding box with love birds and garland border, dated 1988—13" x 8½" basswood.

Illus. 91.

Illus. 92. Plate with American eagle—14"-diameter basswood.

Illus. 93.

Illus. 94. Plate with German eagle, egg-and-dart border, Imperial crown, and Old English lettering—12"-diameter basswood.

Illus. 95. Double-eagle crest from the House of Habsburg.

Illus. 96. Rooster at dawn.

86   FREE-FORM MOTIFS

Illus. 98. Plate with great horned owl—14"-diameter basswood. (Suggested by Jean Lanham.)

Illus. 99.

LETTERING

The tradition of carving letters in works of art probably dates back to the first works of art ever produced. Carving names, dates, initials, and inscriptions on any object satisfies the vanity of both client and artist alike. Even the humble farmer who carved from the human propensity for artistic expression found satisfaction in applying his own name or initials to his work.

Many carving students perceive letter carving as the most difficult task in their learning curriculum. This may be because as children we were coached, drilled, and graded on how to write properly; but when it came to drawing, we were encouraged to express ourselves freely. The fear and anxiety still linger.

The fastest and easiest way to carve letters is the incised method employed in chip carving. The method you use to carve letters is the same as the one applied in executing all other chip carving. The reason this method of carving is easily executed is because you are using a single-edged knife held in a constantly locked position, which is drawn towards you. Carving this way allows greater strength and control, and moves along quickly.

You can choose among any number of lettering styles, for carving. Some, of course, are much easier to execute than others. The real criteria, however, should be how well the lettering style complements the rest of the carving. However, if the project consists of lettering alone, its style should be appropriate for its surroundings. For instance, Roman is a plain lettering style consisting of only capital letters, and it is easy to read (which is why it's so frequently used on plaques and inscriptions). But it may not be appropriate for the architectural style and decor of a church, for which an Old English style might be better suited. If the lettering is to be read from a distance at a glance, its size and legibility should also be considered. If you want to carve a monogram, a script-style lettering would do very nicely. Or, you may desire a plain, readable lettering like Roman but need to use it in a smaller space than that in which Roman will fit. In that case, Ambrosia may be just what you're looking for.

In carving, the lettering styles that show the best are the ones with both wide and narrow features to each letter. Normally, the horizontal part is narrow and the vertical part wide. This causes the letter to appear supported and interesting. In most circumstances, letters cut at all the same width may be technically correct but are usually visually unexciting.

The secret to excellent letter carving really is in the layout. However, with a few general rules to guide you, the mystery soon dissolves and you're on your way to one of the most enjoyable aspects of woodcarving. The most important part of laying out letters is spacing. The most common error made in spacing is placing the letters too far apart. These wide spaces become more apparent when the letters are carved because of shadow depth and the three-dimensional aspect of carved letters. Unless there is some artistic reason for extending the letters in words or names—don't. Take a look at the printing on this page. The letters of each word are so close together that you see and read them as units (words) and not individually. To spread the letters out would force the eye to jump back and forth, making reading difficult and annoying.

There are two ways to space or adjust letters. One is mechanical and the other is artistic (see Illus. 100). The print that you see in newspapers, magazines, and books is generally done with mechanical spacing. Artistic spacing allows you to move those letters that do not inherently fit well together to one side or the other so that they are visually compatible with all the other spacing within a word. For instance, when mechanically spaced, the letters A and V in Roman (and many other types) leave a notable gap. The two letters are far more pleasing when the leg of the V is slid closer to the leg of the A. (Again, see Illus. 100.) Because letters are normally drawn one at a time in preparation for carving, you'll be able to artistically space all your lettering as you go along, which is preferable.

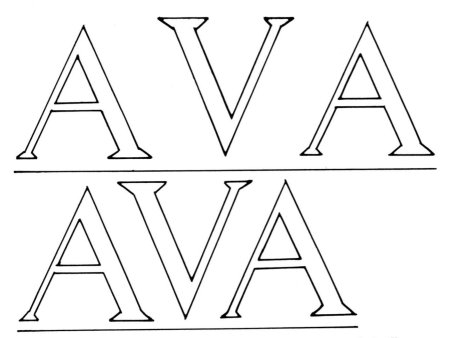

Illus. 100. Top: mechanically adjusted letters. Bottom: artistically adjusted letters.

Though there are always exceptions (as noted above), here are some guidelines to assist you with your spacing. These rules are not chiselled in stone (or wood) and will vary with lettering style and conditions, but they will help you when starting.

- The space between letters is one-half the width of the widest part of the letter, which is usually the vertical leg. For example, if the vertical leg of H is ¼″ wide, the letters of the particular word would be ⅛″ apart.
- The space between words is one-half the height of the capital letter. The space between the period at the end of the sentence and the first word of the new sentence is the full height of the capital. The space between lines of words is one-half the height of the capital. For example, if the capital of a particular type is 1½″, the top of the capitals on the next line will be ¾″ below the first line.
- If you choose one of the more ornate styles of lettering that has very decorative capitals—such as Old English, Becker, or Gothic (all quite similar)—be sure to use both upper- and lowercase. Some make the mistake of using all capitals in order to capture more of the flair offered in these styles. Doing so, however, makes the words difficult, if not impossible, to read and is intrinsically incorrect. A good rule of thumb to follow is

that if a particular lettering style has upper- and lowercase letters, use them both.

- The two styles shown here are Becker and Ambrosia. Both have a nice contrast of wide verticals and narrow horizontals, which makes them excellent choices for carving. Becker is a very legible style with both upper- and lowercase letters. It is a pleasing balance between the simplicity of Roman and decorative Old English. Ambrosia is plain with an artistic flair. It has the added benefit of having narrower letters than most lettering styles, which allows the carving of more letters within a given space. Ambrosia consists of only uppercase letters.

- There are several ways to test for proper spacing. I usually squint at all the lettering as a whole to the extent that I blur the letters beyond recognition. This way, I can immediately see if any letters are spaced too close or too far apart. Another method is to turn your paper around and hold it up to a light so that you can see your lettering from the backside. Because we don't normally read in reverse, looking through the back of a paper blurs the letters and the eye sees only shapes. You will be able to tell immediately whether or not the shapes are spaced correctly.

Illus. 101. Box lid with Ambrosia lettering and floral design—9½" x 7" basswood.

When designing and carving letters, following these simple rules will ensure a good balance and better continuity in your chip carving.

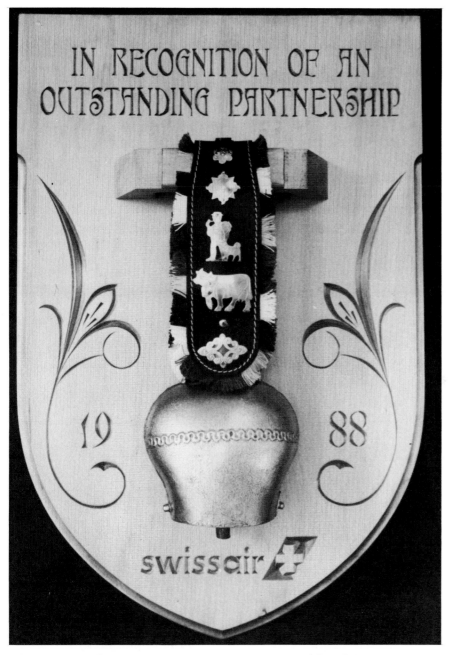

Illus. 102. Wall plaque with Ambrosia lettering—17" x 9" basswood.

ABCDEF

GHIJKLM

NOPQRS

TUVWX

Illus. 103.

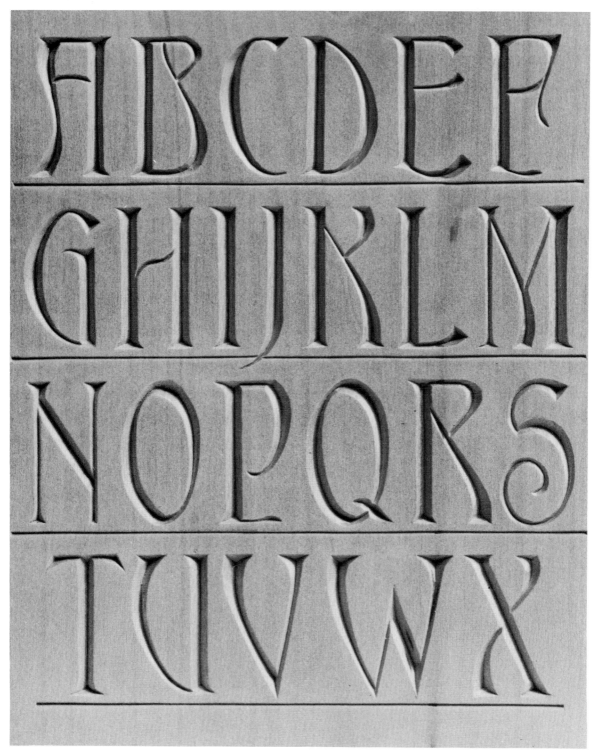

Illus. 104. Ambrosia.

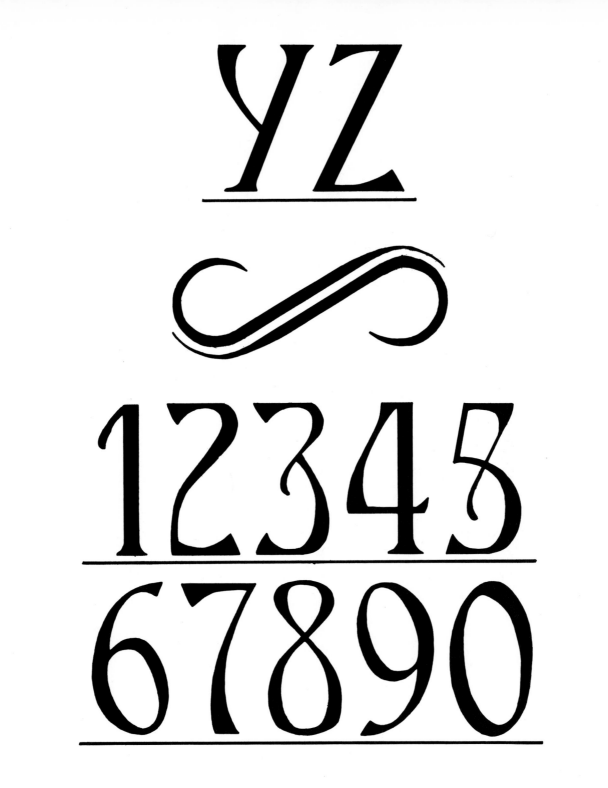

Illus. 105.

Illus. 106. Ambrosia.

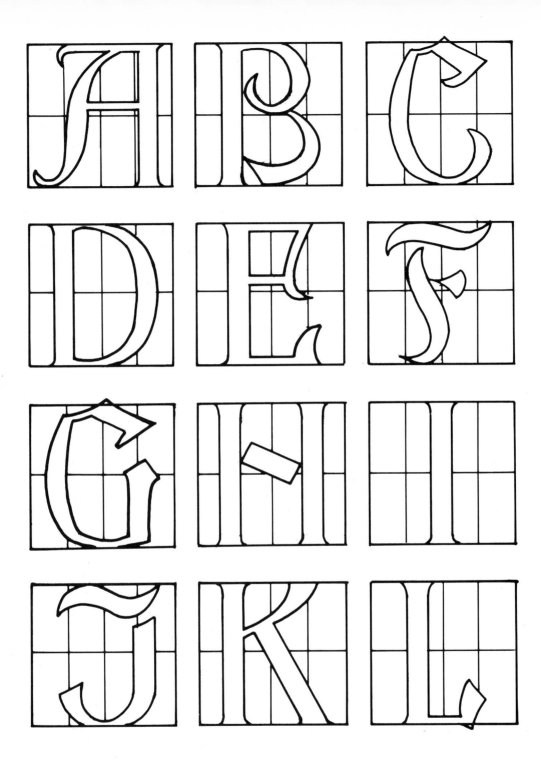

Illus. 107.

Illus. 108. Becker.

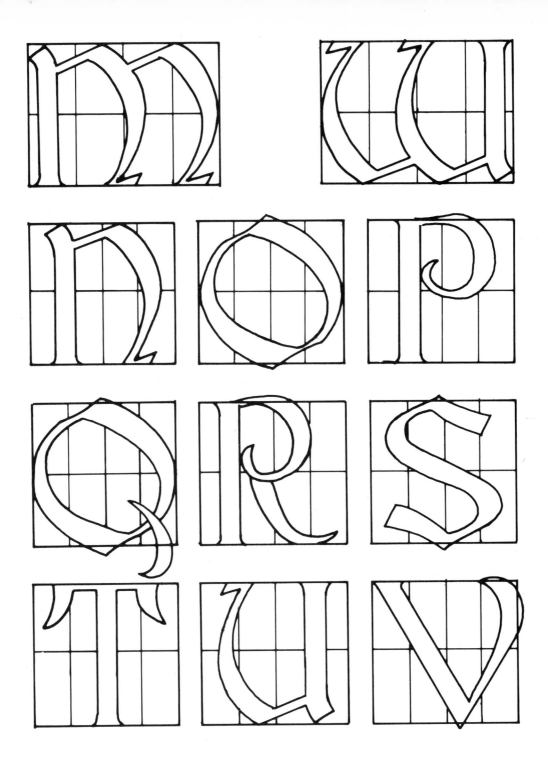

Illus. 109.

Illus. 110. Becker.

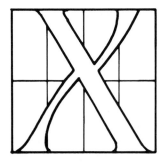
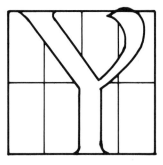
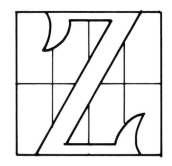

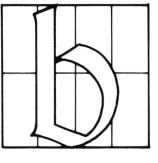
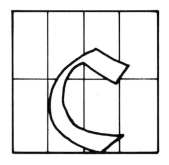

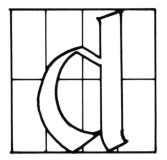
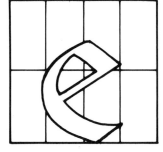
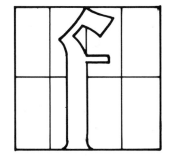

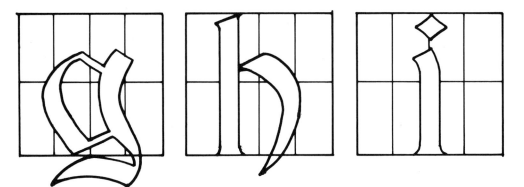

Illus. 111 (above). Illus. 112 (right). Becker.

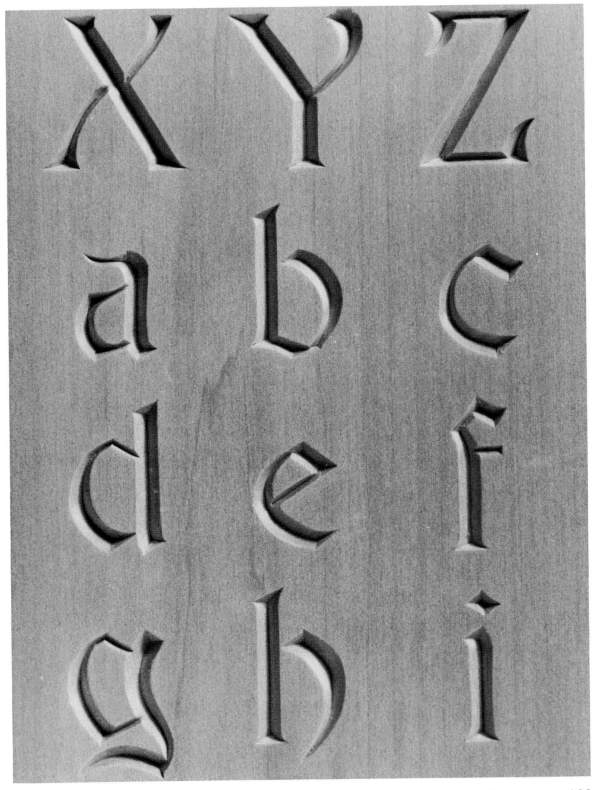

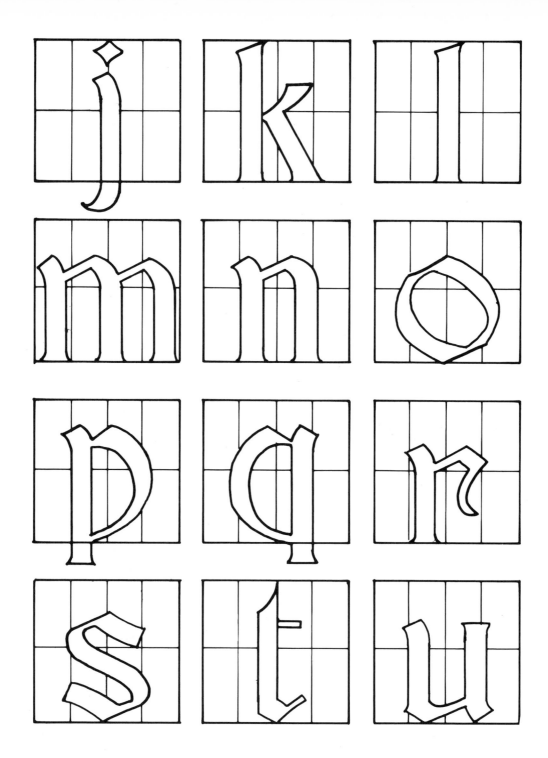

Illus. 113.

Illus. 114. Becker.

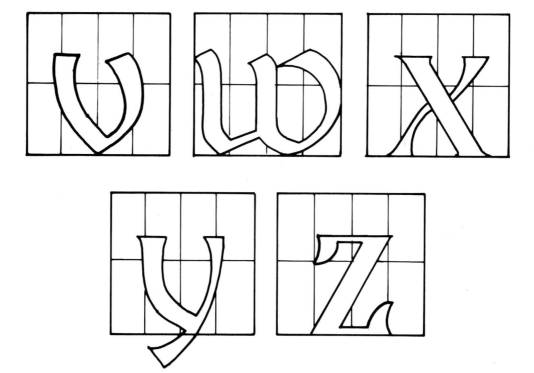

Illus. 115.

Illus. 116. Becker.

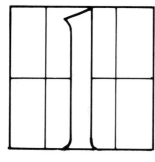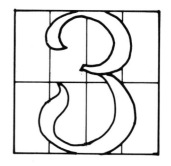

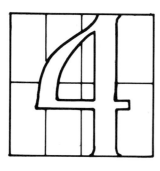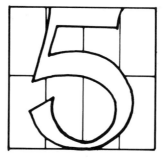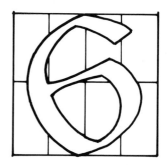

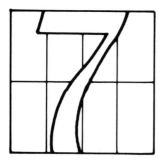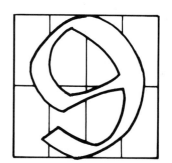

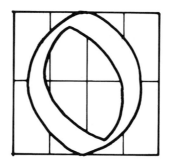

Illus. 117.

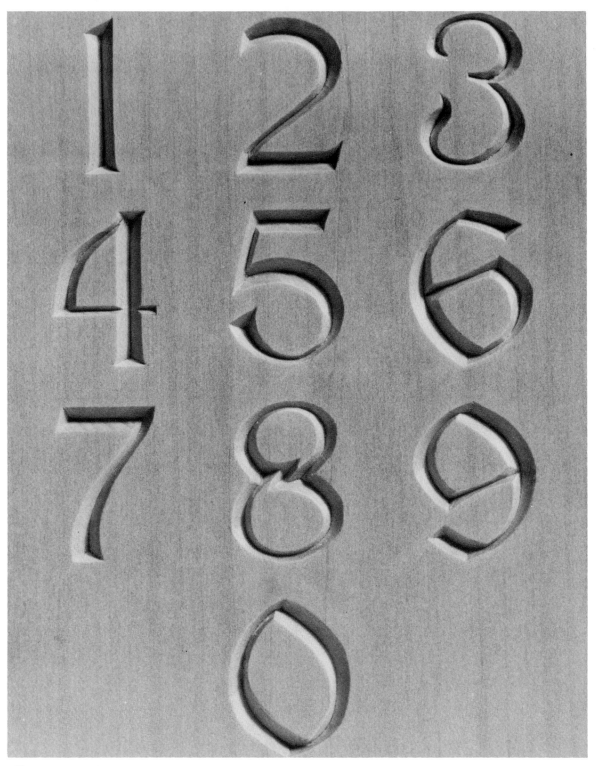

Illus. 118. Becker.

Illus. 119. Box lid with Haverton lettering and double-diamond border—13" x 8½" basswood.

Illus. 120. Box lid with Old English lettering and triple-lace border—13" x 8½" basswood.

Illus. 121. Box lid with Ambrosia lettering and swirl rosette—13" x 8½"
basswood.

Illus. 122. Box lid with Script Monogram LCS and garland
border—9½" x 7" basswood.

FURNITURE CARVING

An exciting way to enhance the appearance of furniture is to carve it. The practice of carving was, and still is, done with traditional furniture in Switzerland as well as in some other European countries. And traditional furniture often is chip-carved.

When designing carving for furniture, the most important consideration should be that the carving fits well on the particular piece of furniture. The carving should not dominate the furniture but rather accent and blend with it so that the carving and the furniture will be seen as one integrated piece. Don't overcarve furniture.

Panels of doors and cabinets are perfect for chip carving, as are drawer fronts, chair backs, clockfaces and a host of other items. Once you start, you'll never look at furniture the same way again. Being able to apply chip carving to furniture is one of the reasons for this craft's growing popularity.

Illus. 123. Hutch—70" high, 60" wide, and 20" deep, of eastern white pine. (Designed and built by Gottlieb Brandli, Swiss Cabinetry, Monroe, WI.) See Illus. 124–134 for details.

Illus. 124. Door panel with Old English B, dated 1986.

Illus. 125. Scalloped border around drawer pull.

Illus. 126.
Egg-and-dart border
around drawer pull.

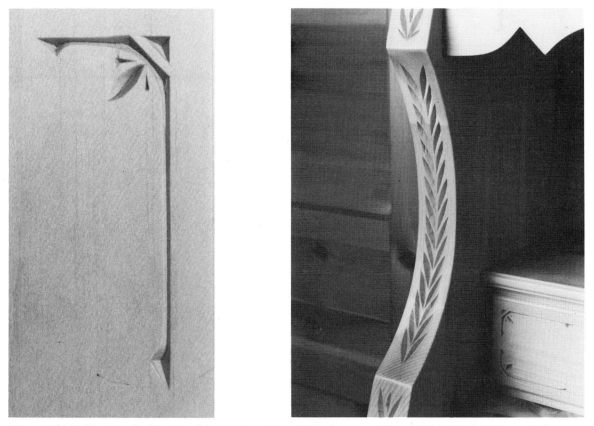

Illus. 127 (left). Simple line border on the edge of the drawer. Illus. 128 (right). Wheat design on the edge of the hutch's side support.

Illus. 129.

Illus. 130. Paisley rosette on door panel—4" diameter.

Illus. 131.

Illus. 132. Floral rosette on door panel—4" diameter.

Illus. 133.

Illus. 134. Floral rosette on door panel—4½" diameter.

Illus. 135. Door panels—eastern white pine. (Designed and built by Gottlieb Brandli.)

Illus. 136. Fifteenth century Norman Gothic hearth stool—18" high, of butternut. (Designed and built by Gottlieb Brandli.)(See Illus. 137–142 for details.)

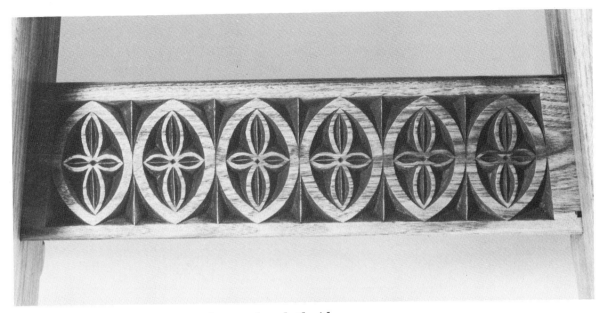

Illus. 137. Trestle of hearth stool, carved on both sides.

Illus. 138. Rosette on seat of hearth stool pierced to make an 8"-diameter handle.

Illus. 139.

Illus. 140. Six-point rosette on side support of hearth stool—4¼″ diameter.

Illus. 141.

Illus. 142. Three-point rosette on side support of hearth stool—4¹/₄″ diameter.

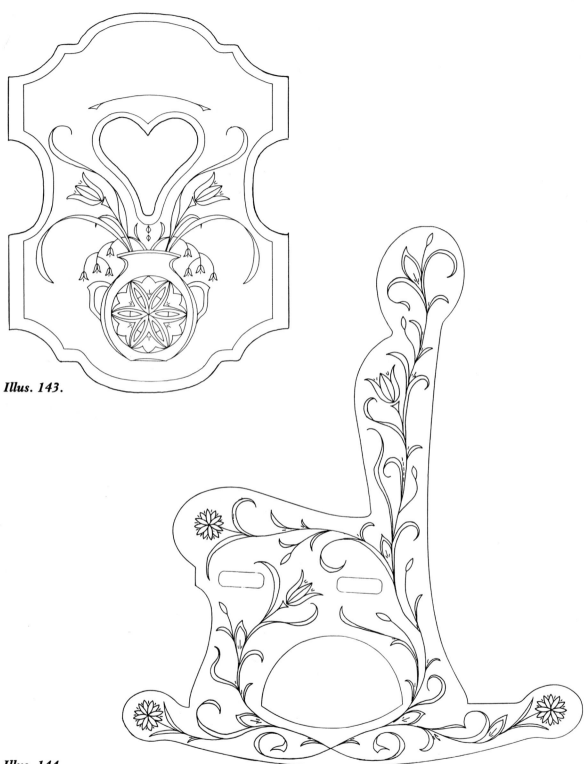

Illus. 143.

Illus. 144.

Illus. 145. Back of child's rocker—of basswood.

Illus. 146. Child's rocker—24″ high, of basswood. (Designed and built by Gottlieb Brandli.)

Index

About the Author

Wayne Barton is an American-born professional woodcarver, who lives in Park Ridge, Illinois, with his Swiss wife, Marlies, and their children. First given an interest in woodcarving at the age of five by his Norwegian grandfather, he has had a serious interest in, and love for, carving all his life.

Mr. Barton took his formal training in Brienz, Switzerland, and his carvings can be found in private collections in Europe and North America. He is the founder and director of the Alpine School of Woodcarving, Ltd., and devotes much of his time to teaching throughout North America and in Switzerland.

Although versed in all disciplines of carving, he specializes in chip carving and has won both national and international awards and recognition for his work.

Acknowledgments

No one truly accomplishes anything alone. Somewhere along the way, someone assists with a word, a deed, a thought, no matter how small. In the writing of this book, there were many who helped in these ways. Standing squarely in the middle are my students, both present and former, as well as a number of participants in the North American carving community who have continually offered encouraging comments and criticism with their friendship.

Outstanding among my students is Robert A. Ostmann. Because of his gracious hospitality, I found myself frequently at his dinner table while he shared with me his broad grasp and understanding of design and chip carving. Apart from my students, most notable is Gottlieb Brandli, who is more knowledgeable about wood and how to work with it than anyone I've ever met. Over many years, he has shared with me his time, wisdom, and ability, with a rare warmth of companionship. His insights and suggestions have been invaluable to me. Nearly all of the pieces shown in this book were designed and built by him.

In terms of the actual writing, I am grateful to my dear friend and secretary, Joanne Inda, who cheerfully endured an endless number of rewrites and assisted in the collating. I am also grateful to Dave Henderson and Carlos Collazo for their professionalism and superb attention to detail in producing nearly all of the photographs.

Most of all, as always, it has been the unfailing assistance and encouragement from my wife, Marlies, that have made this undertaking a reality. I have relied heavily upon her artistic judgment as well as moral support, both of which have made my course wider and straighter. Her unseen energies in this endeavor are enormous. It is with love and gratitude that her contributions are acknowledged.